Pomeranian as Pets

Everything You Need to Know about Pomeranians

Pomeranians Characteristics, Health, Diet, Breeding, Types, Care and a whole lot more!

By Lolly Brown

Disclaimer and Legal Notice

This product is not legal, medical, or accounting advice and should not be interpreted in that manner. You need to do your own due-diligence to determine if the content of this product is right for you. While every attempt has been made to verify the information shared in this publication, neither the author, neither publisher, nor the affiliates assume any responsibility for errors, omissions or contrary interpretation of the subject matter herein. Any perceived slights to any specific person(s) or organization(s) are purely unintentional.

We have no control over the nature, content and availability of the web sites listed in this book. The inclusion of any web site links does not necessarily imply a recommendation or endorse the views expressed within them. We take no responsibility for, and will not be liable for, the websites being temporarily unavailable or being removed from the internet.

The accuracy and completeness of information provided herein and opinions stated herein are not guaranteed or warranted to produce any particular results, and the advice and strategies, contained herein may not be suitable for every individual. Neither the author nor the publisher shall be liable for any loss incurred as a consequence of the use and application, directly or indirectly, of any information presented in this work. This publication is designed to provide information in regard to the subject matter covered.

Neither the author nor the publisher assume any responsibility for any errors or omissions, nor do they represent or warrant that the ideas, information, actions, plans, suggestions contained in this book is in all cases accurate. It is the reader's responsibility to find advice before putting anything written in this book into practice. The information in this book is not intended to serve as legal, medical, or accounting advice.

Foreword

Pomeranian dogs are also known as "Pom" or "Pom – Pom" is a toy breed type of dog and is a delightfully active and aware of everything going on around him. They come from the larger Spitz dogs, specifically the German Spitz. They are very friendly and an ideal companion for all those who want to own a dog. Besides being genuinely friendly, Pomeranian dogs are loyal, very protective and loves being around their owners.

Although Pomeranians are truly a great choice as pets, these dogs doesn't come with a thin instruction manual, but fear not! In this book you'll be easily guided on understanding your Pomeranian dog, their behaviors, their characteristics, how you should feed and care for them and a whole lot more.

Embark on a wonderful journey of sharing your life with a Pomeranian. Learn to maximize the great privilege of living with one and be able to share this unique and unforgettable experience just like many pet owners that came before you!

Table of Contents

Introduction

Pomeranian dogs are the type of dog you would love. They are ideal for small homes and apartments because of their small size. They are very active in indoor places and will do okay without a backyard. Aside from being truly loyal and friendly, Pomeranians are noted for their overwhelming need for human affection and attention.

The Pomeranian's behavior can sometimes be dreadful. They can be reserved with strangers, with excessive barking, and sometimes be growling, be biting and snapping. However, if the owner implies a proper assertion towards the dog, they can be a well-rounded, trustworthy, mentally stable and excellent family companion. It's not a very easy job, mind you, but it's definitely worth it.

The Pomeranians were originally much larger, weighing up to 30 pounds and worked as sheep herders back then. There are still giant Poms that appear today, and they are often called "throwback" Pomeranians.

In 1870, the Kennel Club in England officially recognized them as a breed. In 1888, Queen Victoria started producing them that made the Pomeranian very popular in England.

The life expectancy of Pomeranians is 15 years! They are prone to dislocated patella (kneecap), heart problems, and eye infections, slipped stifle, tooth decay, skin irritations, and early loss. Other names for Pomeranians are Zwergspitz, Dwarf Spitz, Loulou or Pom.

Pomeranian dogs are more than just a pet; it is a loyal, defensive and tender companion. These dogs are trainable, cuddly and energetic, plus they are very great family pets and relates well with children. If you are thinking about adopting a dog or purchasing a puppy, Pomeranians are definitely a great breed to consider. Before you bring a Pomeranians home, however, you should be a responsible dog owner and learn everything you can about this breed and how to care for it properly.

Fortunately, this ultimate guide will teach you on how to be the best Pomeranian dog owner you can be! Inside this book, you will find tons of helpful information about Pomeranian dog; how they live, how to deal with them and realize the great benefits of owning one!

This guide includes information about creating the ideal habitat and diet for your dog as well as tips for breeding and showing your Pomeranian. You will also find in-depth health information for the breed including common health problems affecting it and the treatment options available.

This book is very informative and can direct you on how to be a great Pomeranian owner you would wish to be. Read on!

Glossary of Dog Terms

AKC – American Kennel Club, the largest purebred dog registry in the United States

Almond Eye – Referring to an elongated eye shape rather than a rounded shape

Apple Head – A round-shaped skull

Balance – A show term referring to all of the parts of the dog, both moving and standing, which produce a harmonious image

Beard – Long, thick hair on the dog's underjaw

Best in Show – An award given to the only undefeated dog left standing at the end of judging

Bitch – A female dog

Bite – The position of the upper and lower teeth when the dog's jaws are closed; positions include level, undershot, scissors, or overshot

Blaze – A white stripe running down the center of the face between the eyes

Board – To house, feed, and care for a dog for a fee

Breed – A domestic race of dogs having a common gene pool and characterized appearance/function

Breed Standard – A published document describing the look, movement, and behavior of the perfect specimen of a particular breed

Buff – An off-white to gold coloring

Clip – A method of trimming the coat in some breeds

Coat – The hair covering of a dog; some breeds have two coats, and outer coat and undercoat; also known as a double coat. Examples of breeds with double coats include German Shepherd, Siberian Husky, Akita, etc.

Condition – The health of the dog as shown by its skin, coat, behavior, and general appearance

Crate – A container used to house and transport dogs; also called a cage or kennel

Crossbreed (Hybrid) – A dog having a sire and dam of two different breeds; cannot be registered with the AKC

Dam (bitch) – The female parent of a dog;

Dock – To shorten the tail of a dog by surgically removing the end part of the tail.

Double Coat – Having an outer weather-resistant coat and a soft, waterproof coat for warmth; see above.

Drop Ear – An ear in which the tip of the ear folds over and hangs down; not prick or erect

Entropion – A genetic disorder resulting in the upper or lower eyelid turning in

Fancier – A person who is especially interested in a particular breed or dog sport

Fawn – A red-yellow hue of brown

Feathering – A long fringe of hair on the ears, tail, legs, or body of a dog

Groom – To brush, trim, comb or otherwise make a dog's coat neat in appearance

Heel – To command a dog to stay close by its owner's side

Hip Dysplasia – A condition characterized by the abnormal formation of the hip joint

Inbreeding – The breeding of two closely related dogs of one breed

Kennel – A building or enclosure where dogs are kept

Litter – A group of puppies born at one time

Markings – A contrasting color or pattern on a dog's coat

Mask – Dark shading on the dog's foreface

Mate – To breed a dog and a bitch

Neuter – To castrate a male dog or spay a female dog

Pads – The tough, shock-absorbent skin on the bottom of a dog's foot

Parti-Color – A coloration of a dog's coat consisting of two or more definite, well-broken colors; one of the colors must be white

Pedigree – The written record of a dog's genealogy going back three generations or more

Pied – A coloration on a dog consisting of patches of white and another color

Prick Ear – Ear that is carried erect, usually pointed at the tip of the ear

Puppy – A dog under 12 months of age

Purebred – A dog whose sire and dam belong to the same breed and who are of unmixed descent

Saddle – Colored markings in the shape of a saddle over the back; colors may vary

Shedding – The natural process whereby old hair falls off the dog's body as it is replaced by new hair growth.

Sire – The male parent of a dog

Smooth Coat – Short hair that is close-lying

Spay – The surgery to remove a female dog's ovaries, rendering her incapable of breeding

Trim – To groom a dog's coat by plucking or clipping

Undercoat – The soft, short coat typically concealed by a longer outer coat

Wean – The process through which puppies transition from subsisting on their mother's milk to eating solid food

Whelping – The act of birthing a litter of puppies

Chapter One: Pomeranian in Focus

A dog is a man's best friend, and that being said is right. Pomeranian dogs can be the best friend you would always want; having them by your side to comfort you is bliss! You'll never have to feel alone again whenever you have a Pom, and that's what you called a buddy's friendship! You would love to have a companion whatever or wherever you go. Pomeranian dogs are always there for you. Pomeranian dogs would make the good times better and the hard times easier.

There's nothing as satisfying or as sweet as the unconditional love that they can offer, so then why just stick on a Pomeranian dog. They love to please, and they will be your shadow, your best friend and a whole lot of personality in a little ball of fluff.

Pomeranian dogs are an incredible pet, and you might get excited to have one, but there might be a small chance that this pet is not the right choice for you. Before adopting one, be sure to research and know everything about them so that you would have an excellent idea on what's up ahead.

Pomeranians also have unique names whenever they come in groups. They call a Pom duo a "puff" while a group of three or more is referred to as a "tuft." Okay, I'll give you a minute to sink into that.

Moving on, this chapter will offer all dog lovers the up-to-date information you need to choose, raise, and care for your Pom Poms from puppyhood to its twilight years.

Continue reading on and find out if Pomeranian dogs are really for you. I hope you're ready for more!

Facts about Pomeranian Dogs

Pomeranian dogs are truly fascinating, and you would totally love them just by seeing their physical appearance. They are so fluffy and small, with wedge-shaped heads and little ears. Their appearance resembles a fox because of the shape of their head and muzzle, along with their ever-alert expression. They have a slightly rounded skull, and the eyes are dark in color, but bright and in almond-shaped. Their nose and eye rims are either dark or match the color of their coat. They have a long, thick and coarse coat, with a ruff round neck and chest. Their tail is what makes them different from the rest. They come in various colors such as red, orange, white, or cream, blue brown or black and sometimes their coat is brindle, particolored, or tan pointed.

The weight of Pomeranians on average is from about 3 to 7 pounds. If you looked closely to a Pom, you would notice that they are slightly shorter from shoulder to rear than they are tall, which is measured from the top of the shoulder to the ground.

Poms wear a thick, stand-off double coat with a soft, dense undercoat and a long, straight and harsh topcoat. Its tail is plumed with hair that lies flat and fans out on the dog's back and its neck is covered in longer hair that forms a ruff.

Their tail is something they grow into as they mature that is why Pomeranian puppies are not born with the characteristic tail. Pomeranians appear in just about every color and pattern- blue, blue and tan, black, black and tan, chocolate, chocolate and tan, orange, orange sable, cream, cream sable, red, red sable, white or brindle. Some may come in solid colored or particolored, but there will be no preference given to the show ring to any one color, combination, or pattern.

Each Pom has their personality that makes them unique and admirable. Pomeranians certainly cannot be matched by one or two words that carry over across the entire breed. One unique and interesting characteristic of a Pom is that once they become comfortable with its owner, they will begin to copy their behavior. Let's take this as an example. It the owner is full of energy and very loud, the Pomeranian may mimic that characteristic and will soon become active and vocal. But if the owner tends to be shy and quiet, the Poms will be adapting to a more quiet and relaxed state.

People who live alone are perfect for Pomeranian dogs. They can be a very good companion, usually eager to go for a walk and do different activities together, also, relax and happy to cuddle when at home. Pomeranians are very clingy to their owners that they tend to bond very close to them, but there are some cases that a Pom does not have a close bond with their owner. If that is the case, some extra attention and doing more activities together may be required to make the relationship deep and stronger.

Pomeranians are very protective that they may bark if they sense a stranger or feels there may be impending danger to their owner. They have no fear of anything when they are in 'protection mode.'

A Pom is an indoor dog so whenever you take him out it'll be so fun for him. Consider regularly take your puppy and go out for a stroll; however you should always supervised your dog when they are outside, even if it is in an enclosed area.

Quick Facts

Pedigree: Companion dogs

AKC Group: Toy Group

Breed Size: Small

Height: 8 -11 inches (20 – 28 cm)
Weight: 3 -7 pounds (1.36 – 3 kg)

Coat Length: double coated, thick

Coat Texture: silky, smooth and fine

Color: blue, blue and tan, black, black and tan, chocolate, chocolate and tan, orange, orange sable, cream, cream sable, red, red sable, white or brindle

Ears: small, fluffy

Tail: feathered, long, curled

Temperament: extrovert loves to socialize, loyal, caring

Strangers: generally friendly with strangers as long as there is proper introduction

Other Dogs: generally good with other dogs if properly trained and socialized; may tend to launched itself to larger dogs

Other Pets: friendly with other pets but if not properly introduce may result to potential aggression

Training: active, smart and can be easily trained

Exercise Needs: very active; doesn't require regular or excessive amount of exercise

Health Conditions: cataracts, collapsed trachea, skin problems, distichiasis, entropion, hypoglycemia, luxating patella, pituitary dwarfism, seizues, skin and coat issues

Lifespan: 12 -15 years

History of Pomeranian Dogs

More than with fur and body, Pomeranian dogs boast a surprisingly storied history. Their history is both interesting and educational at the same time. Every owner would want to know a little background of the Pomeranian's origins and ancestry to better appreciate the breed.

Pomeranians originally descended from the Spitz family of dogs in the frozen Arctic region of Iceland. They are much larger than today's Pom because their primary purpose back then are pulling sleds, protecting and hunting. Before, they weighed an average of 30 pounds and were all white, not until the 19th century came when they were bred down to become companion animals. However, as time went by, they were transported to Europe, specifically along Baltic Sea (southern area). This region was called Pomerania which includes parts of today's Poland and Germany. That is where the Pom took its name.

If you're thinking right now why they look like wolves, well yes, because they are closely related to them. They are a spitz breed which means that they have several wolf-like characteristics. There are also other dog breeds that fall from this group such as the Norwegian elkhound, the Alaskan malamute, the Samoyed, and the Akita. They are part of the German Spitzen group, which is a subgroup of the spitz type that is comprised of five different sizes of dogs and Poms belong to the smallest numbers.

Queen Victoria was one of the first ones who owned a Pomeranian. She fell in love with them in the year 1888. The Queen imported more than four Pomeranians from Italy such as Gina (a white female), and Marco which is believed to be a sable colored male. Because of Her Majesty's love for the breed, Pomeranians soon became the era's hottest pet. There came a time that Queen Victoria owned 35 Poms in her kennel, and during her deathbed, she asked for her Pomeranian Turi to be at her side.

Pomeranians have remarkable connections to the history's greatest creative minds like Mozart, who dedicated one of his finished arias to his pet Pomeranian named Pimperl. Also, Frederic Chopin wrote the song "Waltz of the Little Dogs" because he was inspired by his friend's pet Pomeranian chasing his tail. Michelangelo is also one of the historians who had a connection with Poms. His Pom was sitting under a pillow while Michelangelo was painting the Sistine Chapel.

Pomeranian has had a trouble bringing home the bacon on pet shows despite Queen Victoria's cleaning up in competitions. But there was at least one Pom who won Best in Show in the Westminster Kennel Club Dog Show, its name is Great Elms Prince Charming II, who took home top honors in the year 1988.

In 2014, Jiff, a Pomeranian breed made headlines as he set the Guinness World Record for the "Fastest Dog on Two Paws." He ran 10 meters using his hind legs in 6.56 seconds and five meters on his front in 7.76 seconds. But sadly, Jiff's position as the top dog didn't last long, soon after a mixed name Konjo, completely stole the record.

Chapter Two: Pomeranian Requirements

Are you now thinking of getting a Pomeranian dog? Alright! After knowing what they are, their behaviors, and how to deal with them, it's time to give you practical tips on what you need to know before buying one.

In this chapter, you will get a whole lot of information on its pros and cons, its average associated costs as well as the licensing you need so that you will be well on your way to becoming a legitimate Pomeranian pet owner – should you decide to be one! It's up to you! Read on!

License Requirements

Licensing requirements is very important to acquire if you want to own a Pomeranian. In order to apply for a dog license, you need to provide a certificate that shows that your dog is up to date on its rabies vaccinations. Pomeranian dogs that are over four months and older are required to be licensed. If ever you transfer from one place to another, you may need to apply for a new license.

In this section, frequently asked questions regarding Poms' licensing will be discussed so that you will have an idea on the procedures that need to take place before adopting a Pom.

United States Licensing for Dogs

Most major United States' cities require that all dog owners license their dogs. They also require that the dog owners should make sure that the license or tag is always attached to their dog's collars whenever they are in public. There may be fines for dog owners for violating this law.

How much does a dog license cost?

A dog license costs $20 per year for neutered or spayed dogs while for breeds that are not yet spayed or neutered will cost about $34. Dog licenses may be renewed or purchased for 1 to 5 years. All of these fees are non-refundable.

What are the benefits of getting your dog licensed?

- Licensing will definitely help you to be reunited with your dog in case they are lost.
- Your dog can run off-leash in specific cities park dog runs with proof of current dog license and rabies vaccination.
- Licensing can also help reunite the owner and its dog in case of separation during an emergency
- Information about licensed dogs facilitates medical follow-up for individuals that are potentially exposed to infected dogs especially important during rabies breakouts.

The fees of licensing your dogs can provide funding for the city's animal shelter system and free/low-cost neuter and spay programs for low-income dog and cat owners.

When will I receive my dog's license?

You will receive your dog license approximately about two to four weeks after payment is processed. You can also check your application status three weeks after payment is processed by calling 311.

How to renew a dog's license?

You will surely see a notice for renewal in the mail which you can return with payment. You can also do that online if you have an existing license.

How do I replace a lost certificate or license tag?

There is a $1 fee if you want to replace a lost tag. You can also do the replacement process online, or send a written request, though there are no extra charges for replacing a dog license certificate.

Is it important to update my dog's status or my contact information?

It is very vital to keep your contact information updated, and to notify the Health Department if your dog dies or if it changes the owner.

Licensing for Dogs in United Kingdom

In UK, licensing requirements for pets are a little different than they are in the United States. In the United

Kingdom, it is mandatory for dog owners to license their dogs. The main difference, however, is that British dog owners do not need to vaccinate their dogs against rabies because the disease has been eradicated. Dog licenses are renewed annually and they are not a significant expense.

In some cases you will need to get a special permit if you plan to travel with your dog into or out of the country.

Can a Pomeranian Be Left Alone?

A lot of Pomeranian owners cannot be home 24/7, nor can they take their dog with them wherever they go.

When a Pomeranian is left alone by himself, expect your dog to feel isolated. He will undergo extreme sadness, so heavy that the dog suffers intense depression and episodes of anxiety. This may affect the behavior of the dog long after an owner arrives back home.

If you have other responsibilities, whether you go to school or work that take you away from the house, a dog of 8 weeks and older will be able to be home alone for 8 to 9 hours given that he has the right set-up for comfort, safety and to meet all of his needs.

It will take an effort and a bit of careful planning to ensure that your Pomeranian dog is protected, won't get into any trouble, can reach both his water and food and has the right things to help keep stress and anxiety at a minimum.

Additionally, it is possible to train a Pomeranian to gain more self-confidence about being by himself and to also learn how to be independent which is a huge part of handling the isolation.

It is never recommended to leave a Pomeranian at home for longer than 8 to 9 hours because as time flies, there is a greater chance of something happening. Food and water can run out, poo and pee will accumulate in the dog's designated area, etc.

If you will be gone longer than 8 to 9 hours, or overnight, it is better to have your Pomeranian stay with a friend or family member. There is also an alternative to placing your Poms in a doggie day care or canine hotels for overnights.

How Many Pomeranians Should You Keep?

There are several important factors you need to consider when answering this question. The question is do you have the space and the financial ability to provide for more than one dog? Poms are small, and generally a low maintenance breed but they still require a good deal of time and attention – think carefully before buying more than one of them. If you do have the time and money to care for another dog, your Pom might appreciate having another dog of its kind around to keep him company while you are away.

Ideally one or two Pom dogs are fine; just make sure that before you get another one, you can provide for the needs of both dogs. As long as you socialize your Pom from a young age, they shouldn't have trouble getting along with each other or with other dogs.

Do Pomeranians Get Along with Other Pets?

For the most part, Poms get along with other pets as long as they have been properly socialized from a young age, however these dogs as small as they are, are not aware of their own size that's why they tend to launch themselves towards bigger dogs such as Great Pyrenees, Labrador etc. In order to prevent potentially disastrous consequences, introduce your dog to larger dogs under supervision, before they interact on their own. It is also important to note that huge dogs shouldn't be around smaller ones because they seem them as prey.

If you are going to have other household pets around such as cats, it is wise to properly introduce them and also monitor their interaction to make sure they're getting along. Be more cautious when introducing strangers, even if dogs are man's best friend, they still might be sensitive to new faces, so do it properly.

Ease and Cost of Care

All of us love our pets, but let's be honest- they can be expensive. But no matter how expensive your dog may be, it is just a drop in the bucket if you compare it to how much you'll be spending over the next few weeks, months, and years with them.

The cost of owning a Pomeranian dog is an extremely important consideration for a number of often overlooked reasons. Adopting a Pom requires a financial commitment for its health and well-being. It can be really expensive so you should prepare financially for their healthcare, grooming, training classes, food, toys, treats, boarding, and other expenses.

Pomeranian dogs do cost money, and before entering into an emotional relationship with it, you should already be prepared to pay for the care that your pet will require. If you cannot afford to provide financially the proper care for a Pom, please do not get one.

This section of the book will give you an idea on how much you should invest on Pomeranian dogs. Of course, owning one means providing for its necessities such as the food and treats, cleaning supplies, grooming, toys, veterinary care, and some other costs.

Initial Costs

There are initial costs of owning a dog and it is extremely important to considerate for a number of often overlooked reasons. Some of these expenses are initial adoption fees, monthly food bills, vaccinations, vet visits, chew toys, etc.

This section will elaborate all the expenses that you will spend in keeping a Pomeranian dog.

Purchase Price: starts at $500 to $1200

The initial cost of buying a purebred Pomeranian will be very important in your decision making process, and of course, the cost of care should be also considered.

Take note that the price will depend on several factors that will be explained below-

- **Cost based on where the Pom came from**

The cost of a Pom varies on which section of the country the breeder resides. Depending on where you live, there can be a scarce or a lot of available Poms available. Let's take this for example. In New England, there are few Pomeranian breeders if you compared it to other states. So this means that to locate a quality, Poms coming from a small home breeder will definitely cost more than from a state in which there are a larger number of Pom pups available.

- **The time of the year**

Timing is everything so that is absolutely true when buying a Pomeranian. The cost of a Pom comes down during the months that we do not think about bringing a new Pom home. That being said, in places such as this, there is a high demand during spring and summer months and a lower demand during winters.

- **Age**

    The recommended time to sell a Pom is between 6 weeks old (when a Pom is chosen and a deposit is placed down) to 8 weeks old. This will be the age in which most pups are ready to transition to their new homes. The notion of adopting a 2-month-old is rooted in people's minds, that when a Pom passes that age, the cost is greatly reduced in an effort to sell the Pom before it reached 3 or 4 months. The time demand lowers quite a bit and because of that, a breeder will find that no one is interested in obtaining a Pom of that age.

- **Color**

    It is amazing that Pomeranians can be found in such a wide range of different colors. The most common are orange but there are also some colors which are already rare such as blue and even lavender. Of course, the rarer a color or a coat combination, the higher will be the cost.

- **Type of registration**

It is recommended to obtain an AKC Pomeranian although there are many CKC registered Poms that are perfectly healthy and can make a great pet. The reason why AKCs are recommended is because they are strict about rules and regulations. For example, visits are only done at the premises in order to ensure that the program stays small. It is definitely more expensive for a breeder to offer AKC pups. Therefore, this means that the price for a registered AKC Pom will generally be higher than a CKC. However, it is of high recommendation that this is worth the cost increase.

Therefore, adopting a Pomeranian dog requires a financial commitment for its overall health and well-being. In the below section, it will give you a rough idea of how big a commitment you should plan on getting a Pom. These costs are based on surveys from pet parents around the country. Take note that some may be higher or lower depending on the place where you live.

An overview of the initial costs is provided for you in on the next section, this includes other materials that you pet will need for maintenance. Costs may vary depending on brand as well as location and the current exchange rate.

General Expenses Overview

Needs	Costs
Purchase Price	$500 - $1,200 (£400.45 - £961.08)
Crate	$30 (£19.50)
Food/Water Bowl	$20 (£18)
Toys	$50 (£32.50)
Microchipping	$30 (£19.50)
Vaccinations	$50 (£32.50)
Spay/Neuter	$50 to $200 (£32.50 - £130)
Accessories	$35 (£32.50)
Total	$ 765 to $1,580 (£612.69 - £1265.42)

Monthly Costs

The monthly costs associated with keeping a Pomeranian can also be quite expensive. Some of the things that need to be bought on a monthly basis are food and treats, annual license renewal, toy replacements, and veterinary exams. Provided in this section is an overview of each of these costs as well as an estimate for each cost.

Food and Treats: total of $50 (£32.50)

Feeding your Pomeranian a healthy diet is very important for its health and wellness, especially for a very active and huge pet. A high-quality diet for dogs may not be cheap and highly depends on the brand. The right amount of nutrients should be provided to maintain its healthy and appealing physique. You should be prepared to spend around $40 for a high-quality dog food which will last you about a month. You should also include a monthly budget of at least $10 for treats, that way he/she can be rewarded every time he/she did a good job in training or behaving.

Grooming Costs: approximately $9 to $12.50 (£8 - £11.25)

You should plan to have your Pomeranian professionally groomed about twice a year in order to keep his skin and coat in good health. You should budget about $10.50 (£8 - £11.25) per month.

License Renewal: average of $2.00 (£1.30)

The cost to license your Pomeranian is generally about $20 and you can renew the license for the same price each year, some states may cost more. License renewal cost divided over 12 months is about $2 per month.

Veterinary Exams: approximately $7.00 (£4.55)

In order to keep your Pomeranian healthy you should take him to the veterinarian at least twice a year; keep in mind that you may need to take him more often while he is a puppy to give him the vaccines he needs. The average cost for a vet visit is about $40 (£26) so, if you have two visits per year, it averages to about $7 (£4.55) per month.

Additional Costs: $15 (£9.75)

In addition to the cost for food, grooming, license renewal, and vet visits you will have to cover other costs on occasion. These costs may include replacements for toys, a larger collar as your puppy grows, cleaning products, and more. You won't have to cover these costs every month but you should include it in your budget to be safe.

An overview of these costs is provided for you in on the next section. Costs may vary depending on brand as well as location and the current exchange rate.

Monthly Expenses Overview

Needs	Monthly Costs
Food and Treats	$50 (£32.50)
Grooming Costs	$9 to $12.50 (£8 - £11.25)
License Renewal	$2 (£1.30)
Veterinary Exams	$7 (£4.55)
Other Costs	$15 (£9.75)
Total	$83 to $95.50 (£68.09 – £78.34)

Pros and Cons of Pomeranian Dogs

<u>Pros</u>

- Pomeranians are really very cute and they are known as a "big personality in a little dog"
- Pomeranians come in small sizes that make it advantageous to meet size limitations for airplanes and hotels
- Pomeranians are very active and they can simply just get their exercise even while staying indoors.

- Pomeranians do not need to consume a lot of space that makes them great for apartments.
- Pomeranians are very light, weighing 3-10 lbs, which makes them easy to carry around wherever you go.
- Pomeranians, because of their small size, are less prone to break items in your house.
- Pomeranians won't be able to drag you around whenever you give them a walk because they are so light.
- Pomeranians are cheaper to feed, house and medicate compared to larger breeds

Cons

- Pomeranians are very fragile that they can be seriously injured or even be killed if they jump off small walls.
- Purebred Pomeranians can be quite expensive to buy because of their popularity.
- Pomeranians can be easily injured by other animals such as birds.
- Pomeranians really shed a lot and require daily grooming.
- Pomeranians can be very prone to barking like many other small breed dogs.
- Pomeranian is not a good choice for children because small children may handle them roughly.

- Pomeranians can be stubborn and smart so they can test your patience. This characteristic of them was developed because they descended from northern working dogs.
- Since Pomeranians are very small in sizes, they can be able to go to small spaces and because their poop and pee stains are relatively small too, they could hide these in nooks and crannies without you knowing it. This will make your housebreaking more challenging.
- Pomeranian owners can easily give in to "small dog syndrome", wherein they pamper the small dog a lot that he believes he is the head of the pack. You should take in mind that dogs are pack animals so understanding this psychology is necessary for training them properly.

Chapter Three: Tips in Buying Pomeranian Dogs

Now that you've reached this point, I assume you are ready to purchase a Pomeranian dog. It is very exciting for you and your family to be making the long-term commitment in owning a Pom. When thinking about purchasing this dog, there are a few things you need to take in consideration.

This chapter will give you tips and advice to make the best decision in choosing a Pomeranian dog. This will be an overview in finding the right dog and finding the right breeder.

Finding a Reputable Pomeranian Breeder

Once you've decided that the Pomeranian is the right dog for you, your next step is to find one. Purchasing a Pomeranian might be as easy as stopping in to your local pet store since it is such a popular breed, but you should ask yourself whether this is really the best option. Many pet stores receive their puppies from puppy mills – organizations which breed dogs as quickly as they can, keeping the dogs in squalid conditions. As a result of irresponsible breeding practices, the puppies are often malnourished or suffering from health problems. The best way to make sure you get a Pomeranian puppy in good health is to do your research and to purchase one from a reputable Pomeranian breeder.

Tips in Choosing a Reputable Breeder

The difference between a reputable breeder and a puppy producer is that the former spends large amounts of time and money on the best interest of the breed, while the latter is often motivated by profit. However, in order to find a good Pomeranian breeder, you may have to do some research first. Once you've compiled a list of several Pomeranian breeders you then need to go through them to choose the best option. You don't want to run the risk of purchasing a puppy from a hobby breeder or from someone who doesn't follow responsible breeding practices. Keep in mind that when you purchase a Pomeranian puppy you are making a 15 year commitment!

Here are the following things you need to do to help you find a reputable Pomeranian breeder:

- Ask around at veterinary offices, groomers, and pet stores for referrals to Pomeranian breeders and assemble as much information as you can about each one.

- Visit the website for each breeder (if they have one) and check to see if the breeder is registered with a national or local breed club

- Contact each breeder individually and ask them questions about their knowledge of the Pomeranian breed as well as their breeding experience.

- Ask specific questions about the breeder's program and the dogs used to produce the puppies. Ask what the breeder does to prevent the passing of congenital conditions to the puppies.

- Remove the breeders from your list who do not seem to be knowledgeable about the breed or if they seem to be just hobby breeders looking to make a buck.

- Eliminate breeders from your list who refuse to answer your questions or who do not seem genuinely concerned for the wellbeing of their puppies.

- Schedule a visit with several breeders and ask for a tour of the facilities – check to make sure they are clean and that the dogs look healthy.

- Narrow down your list of breeders and make your selection – you should also ask about the breeder's preferences for putting down a deposit on a puppy.

- Place your deposit to reserve a puppy – in the next section you will receive tips for choosing a puppy from a litter.

Rescue Dogs Adoption

As an alternative to purchasing a Pomeranian puppy from a legitimate breeder, you should also consider adopting a rescue dog. Not only will you be doing your part in the war against puppy mills, but you will be providing a homeless dog with a loving home and new lease on life. There are many benefits associated with adopting a rescue dog and you might even be able to find a purebred Pomeranian or a Pomeranian puppy.

Adoption is much more affordable than purchasing a purebred puppy from a breeder and the dog is likely to have already been housebroken and may also have some amount of obedience training as well.

List of Breeders and Rescue Websites

In this section, you'll be given recommended websites on reputable breeders as well as rescue dogs associations in United States and United Kingdom, once you have narrow down your list of breeders, you can go and check to see the best option for you.

U.S. Pomeranian Breeders

Puppy Spot
<https://www.puppyspot.com/breed/pomeranian/?breed_id=238&page=1>

Canton Pomeranians
<http://www.cantonpomeranians.com/>

Chars Poms
<http://www.charspoms.com/>

Finch's Poms
<http://www.finchspoms.com/>

Parker's Precious Pomeranians
<http://www.parkerspreciouspoms.com/>

U.S. Pomeranian Recues

Rescue Me
<http://pomeranian.rescueme.org/>

Ohio Pom Rescue
<http://www.ohiopomrescue.com/>

Recycled Pomeranians and Schipperkes
<http://www.recycledpomeranians.com/>

Adopt-a-Pet
<http://www.adoptapet.com/s/adopt-a-pomeranian>

U.K. Pomeranian Breeders

The Kennel Club
<https://www.thekennelclub.org.uk/services/public/acbr/Default.aspx?breed=Pomeranian>

Altina Pomeranian UK
<http://www.altina.co.uk/>

Mini Pomeranians
<http://www.minipomeranians.co.uk/>

Paavali Pomeranian
<http://www.paavali.co.uk/>

PommaniaPoms
<http://pommaniapoms.com/>

Chelliche

<http://www.chelliche.co.uk/>

U.K. Pomeranian Rescues

Dog's Trust
<https://www.dogstrust.org.uk/>

Blue Cross UK
<https://www.bluecross.org.uk/>

Royal Society for the Prevention of Cruelty to Animals UK
<https://www.rspca.org.uk/home>

Little Dog Rescue UK
<http://www.littledogrescue.co.uk/index.html>

Many Tears Rescue UK
<http://www.manytearsrescue.org/>

Tips on Purchasing a Pomeranian

Your chosen Pomeranian will be part of your family for an extended period so make sure to select the right dog for your family. Remember to not impulsively purchase that cute puppy in the window of your local pet shop to avoid many of the problems experienced by new puppy owners and save yourself a lot of heartaches. If you want to own a pet, escape from impulse buying.

It is recommended to purchase your Pomeranian puppy from a trusted and reputable, registered show Pomeranian breeder. It is very simple to select a dedicated breeder. Be sure also to avoid a registered backyard. Just ask if either the parent of the Pom is a champion and how many wins the breeder has bred. Also, ask the number of years the breeder has been showing their Pomeranians. This will give you the best opportunity of obtaining a companion who is a true representative of its breed. Never be fooled into purchasing a Pom from a registered backyard breeder. It is recommended that you must research the Pom breed thoroughly before buying.

The following are the questions you should ask the breeder before buying the Pom:

- Ask to see and visit the puppy and the parents in the breeder's home
- Ask to see both the parents because this will give you an idea of how the puppy will be as an adult. Do not buy a Pom from a breeder that refuses to allow you to come to their place and see the parents of the Pom.
- If you are buying online, ask for more photos of the puppy at different angles to make sure it is not a scam. Also, ask to forward the photos of the parents to you.

- Ask questions about the size of the Pom now. A good breeder can tell you the puppies' current weight.
- Also, ask the breeder how much grooming and exercise the Pom will require.
- Ask about any health problems. Has the Pom been vet checked? Are they wormed on regular basis? Has the Pom been micro chipped?
- Ask if the parents of the puppy are DNA profiled.
- Ask if the breeder has been involved in Pomeranian rescue. Only purchase a puppy from a breeder who is dedicated to the breed.
- Ask if the breeder belongs to a Breed Club or Association. In the United States, puppies should be registered with the AKC (American Kennel Club). Take note, you must only purchase AKC registry puppies. This is because the AKC has strict rules of requirements and membership from the breeders. This rule is a good safeguard for a dog buyer.
- Ask if the breeder has a contract. A reputable breeder will have a contract that must spell out all conditions of sale.
- Ask if the breeder has a website. Most good breeders have a website. Also, be sure to avoid breeders who offer credit card or other easy payment methods online, including PayPal. Beware of the breeders who are in a hurry to sell their pet and close the deal.

If you are really interested in purchasing a Pomeranian dog, whether it is adult or puppy, do not hesitate to visit the Pomeranian Directory. It lists the very best Pomeranian breeders, AKC Registered Pomeranian Breeders and Reputable Kennel Club.

Selecting a Healthy Pomeranian

A Pomeranian breed is very prone to certain canine health problems and diseases. I am not telling that your Pom will get these diseases but you must be aware that your dog is healthy so it will not be difficult to take care of them.

Keeping an eye for early signs of medical problems of your dog is of utmost importance; it could save you a lot of stress, time and money in the long run – not to mention your dog's health. This section will give you information if your Pomeranian dog is healthy to keep.

- **Monitor their eating habits**

    If your dog ignores his drink or food for more than 24 hours, you must see a vet immediately, especially if your dog is usually a big eater.

- **Do a body check**

    You should be doing a full body check of your dog on a weekly basis. You can gently run your hand over all the parts of your dog's body and check for cuts, lumps, inflammation and any signs of discomfort.

- **Observe on their walking**

    Watch the way your dog moves when you're out on walks. Observe how he walks and runs. Does he ever seem stiff? Get easily tired? Or have a limp? Excessive panting and coughing may also indicate problems

- **Check their weight**

    You should avoid obesity. This is the cause of a large number of problems in dogs. You should keep your dog on a steady, well-balanced diet. Seek advice sooner if things start to get out of control rather than later.

- **Monitor their toilet habits**

Constipation, diarrhea, blood and mucus are the four things to look out for in your stool of your dog. Also, if the urine is dark, blooded or cloudy, then you must already be sensitive on that. Keep an eye on their toilet habits and make sure it is regular. Be sure also that the appearance is consistent.

- **Check their mouth**

Check your dog's mouth for anything out of the ordinary. Gums must be pink. If you see darker/redder patches, it may indicate a problem. You must also check for growths and lumps, and make sure that the teeth are clear. Observe also their breath as unusually bad breath could be an indication of digestive problems.

- **Check their eyes**

Eyes of dogs should be clear and the pupils should be of the same size. Check for ingrowing hair or eye lashes that look like it's causing a problem. Make sure also that there is no excessive discharge or signs of irritation. Visit a vet if there is.

- **Check their nose**

  The nose of dogs should be cool and moist. Keep an eye out for excessive sneezing, discharge and make sure that breathing is unobstructed and easy.

- **Check their feet**

  Scrutinize your dog's feet for any grazes, cuts or growths. Long nails may cause problems and should be trimmed, either with file or dog clippers. You have to be careful when cutting the nails of your dogs to avoid bleeding.

- **Check their ears**

  Lastly, check the ears of your dogs for wax build-up, bad odor, and swelling. Wax can be easily removed if done properly. Use cotton wool but you should never poke anything directly down your dog's ears.

  This basic checklist should be properly observed and performed on a regular basis. Doing so will ensure that you catch any sign of trouble as early as possible. Always remember that if anything looks different on your Poms, never hesitate to consult your vet.

Chapter Four: Caring Guidelines for Pomeranian Dogs

This chapter will give you a lot of tips and advice on how to take care of your Pomeranian dog. You will have an idea on how to train, groom and clean them plus, you will get some nice tips if you want to present them in a show. There are still a lot of important things you need to know about your Pomeranian dogs so continue reading on and find out more about your cute fluffy dog.

Socializing Your Dog

The best time to socialize your Pom is when they are, in fact, a pup. Dogs are at their most receptive and sensitive between three and twelve weeks of age. The earlier you can get your dog socialized, the better. After those span of twelve weeks, it can be very difficult to get a puppy to accept anything unfamiliar.

- **Walk your dog daily** – introduce them to other dogs
  Dog walks have a great advantage in meeting new dogs and people as well as practice their proper behavior when they are out because you're just bound to run into more social situations when your dog is out for a walk than when staying at home.

- **Use a muzzle when other dogs come over**
  If you already know that your Pom barks or growls at other dogs, it can help if you let them use a muzzle. This prevents the danger of attacking or biting and it can also make the dogs calmer so they'll be more sensitive to meeting other dogs and have a more positive experience.

- **Expose your dogs to different social activities**

    If you can introduce your dog to a new activity once a week, it will go a long way in helping them socialize, be calm and more behaved.

Training Your Pomeranian Dogs

    The good thing about Pomeranians is that they are very good with training; whether it is for heeling, housebreaking or performing tricks.

    Training is a combined effort between the owner and the dog. The owner will take the important role of a teacher, while your Pom will be the great student. Pomeranians are pretty fast learners but it may take longer based on some other factors.

    Two of the most important things to be considered will be how strictly you will be to stick with the training and how many learning opportunities your Pom have.

    A lot of these things depend on you, as an owner. It will be important for you to understand and follow the housebreaking guidelines and a big part of this will be how often times your dog has a chance to train his lessons.

Potty training

A lot of owners believe that toy breed dogs can easily be trained to use a litter box or pee pads. This is not as easy as it sounds, but it is still possible. Poms may have a hard time using pee pads because they have a natural instinct to want to choose on the right spot to pee or poop.

However, indoor training can be easily done if you are persistent and if you have a cooperative, Pom.

There should be a chosen spot as the 'designated bathroom area' and this will be the term used whether you have pee pads in a corner that is already set up or have an indoor grass mat for your Pom.

Preparing to Housebreak Your Pomeranian

- **Choose the designated area**

Take note that you should never allow your Pom to go outside somewhere. There should be one certain area to be chosen as designated bathroom area. Ideally, it will be an area that ranges from 8 to 10 foot in diameter.

- **Choose a containment method**

A Pom that is not fully housebroken should never be free in either a room or the house especially if he is not well supervised.

- **Choose your reward treats**

A Pom is going to be more motivated to focus, be able to soak in the training, understand that he did something right, and look forward to the next training lesson if he is properly rewarded with treats.

- **Be ready for a speedy exit**

To have your Pom wearing his collar and to keep the leash right by the door is the final step in preparing to facilitate a fast exit to the designated area. It is highly recommended to have a harness. If you are not used to having one, you may at first think that they are difficult to take on and off.

You are already ready to housebreak your Pom successfully once you.

- Have chosen the best location for your dog's designated bathroom area that will be relatively easy to reach.
- Have set up a playpen or some other containment method for your dog to be at any time you can't keep an eye on him
- Have special training treats right by the exit door and have your dog's harness on him and his leash that is ready to spring into action

Housebreaking Tips

- Keep your Pom with you, as often as possible. If he will pee or poo, clap your hand loudly or call out his name to cause him to pause.
- Your prep should allow you to exit with your dog quickly, but carry him if needed.
- As your Pom is doing the deed, repeat a chosen word or phrase so that he can associate it with his actions. Some owners use 'bathroom' or 'piddy potty'.
- Bring your Pom outside with a specific schedule. If you are heading to the yard to get some exercise, bring him to his bathroom area first.
- Allow your Pom at least 15 minutes to find the perfect spot within the area, and for his bladder and bowel muscles to relax.
- If your Pom is done peeing, offer the reward treat right away. Always give praise to them at the same time.
- If there are in some cases that accidents happen in the house, it is important to clean the area with an enzyme cleanser. This is because it might be announced to your Pom that 'This is the bathroom area'

Behavioral Problems

Active, intelligent, and a relatively healthy breed, Pomeranians make a great companion and also do well in competitions, including obedience and agility trials. However, some Poms may be prone to specific behavioral problems, so potential owners should consider the temperament of these dogs before adopting one.

Aggression and Fear

Poms tend to be suspicious around strangers and they become intimidated to large people and animals because of their small size. Fear can turn to aggression and you should not consider your dog's fear as an endearing behavior.

Possessiveness and Territoriality

Pomeranians are likely to be possessive of toys and food because they have a strong reputation for being demanding to owners. You should train them by putting your hand in their bowl and playing toy exchange games when she is a puppy. This will decrease the likelihood of territorial behavior in adulthood

Excessive barking

Poms are notoriously yappy dogs, especially when they are not socialized to strangers and loud noises. You can put your dog in a crate when they bark excessively loud and reward them for being calm and quiet when there are visitors.

Grooming Pomeranian Dogs

In regards to grooming, Pomeranians are on the higher level of maintenance. If grooming is not performed properly or on a regular basis, things can go out of control. The coat can become matted. Fur may become brittle. The skin may dry out. Tear stains might become excessive. Paws and nose might peel. In short, it can become a disaster.

Regular Pomeranian Grooming Tips

- **Toenails**

Make sure to clip your Pom's toenails with dog toenail clippers once every six or eight weeks. It will keep your dog's paws clean and healthy and will prevent him from scratching upon jumping up. Be sure not to cut their nails too close as this may hurt them.

- **Teeth**

You have to thoroughly brush your Pomeranian's teeth on a regular basis as this type of breed is prone to dental cavities. You have to use special toothpaste that contains enzymes to inhibit bacterial growth in the mouth.

- **Eyes**

Pomeranians tend to have a lot of discharge from their eyes that may cause an infection due to bacteria. Hence, it is important to clean the eye area of your Pom.

- **Trimming**

Your Pomeranian does not need to be shaved down during hot weather. There is no reason to shave your Pom's beautiful coat just because the weather is hot. It is because if the inner layer is shaved, it may never grow back again to once it was before. Little touch-ups to keep things clean and neat can be done every 2 to 3 months as needed.

Show Dog Pomeranian Training

You can go far beyond basic commands in training Pomeranian if you are committed and if you really wanted it to. Poms are very well known for their exceptional learning skills. This makes them an ideal breed for the show ring.

The following information will give you an idea on how to use the right Pomeranian training to prepare your Pom to become a show dog.

- You need to understand the first aspect of training for a show is that it requires a lot of hard work. Unlike teaching your Pom basic commands, the lessons need to be taught are activities training.
- You should learn how to properly groom your Pom for a show. You can get it from a professional book, from a video or from a groomer itself.

You should make grooming an enjoyable experience just like Pomeranian training. It helps to get your Pom used to grooming because this will help him become more accustomed to being handled.

- Practice posing or stacking your dog as soon as he is comfortable with the grooming table. First, have him stay in his position for a few seconds. And then increase the time you make him stay on the table. Be sure to give him a lot of rewards for standing poised for a long period of time.

Once your dog knows how to stay poised, you can move to the next step of his training which is the inspecting your Pom as a judge will. You have to check his legs, teeth, feet, etc.

- You can enroll your Pom in handling classes
- Your dog will need leash training. This form of training is about putting him on a leash and then eventually allowing him to go wherever he wants.

Once your Pom is already familiar with changing directions, the next thing is to teach him on a loose head. Your dog will be taught to stand beside you when you stop, and then your dog will walk beside you, right or left side.

- You can also attend conformation training classes. These are to mirror show conditions, which make them an ideal place for show training. These classes will surely help you learn and fine tune all the skills that are required in a show ring.

Finally, before deciding to enter your Pom in a dog show, you should first attend a few shows so you can have an idea. The more you and your dog are prepared for a show, the more your training will pay off.

Chapter Five: Nutritional Needs of Pomeranian Dogs

The right way of feeding your Pomeranian is very essential in his overall health. How, how much, and how often are vital questions that needs to be answered in terms of feeding your Poms. Pomeranian puppies need the right amount of nutrition to grow, adults need the best diet to maintain health and senior Poms need the right food possible to meet the needs of an older dog.

This section will elaborate all the tips on how to feed your Poms and the basic nutritional needs that they require in order to have a healthy immune system.

Tips for Feeding Your Pomeranians

Different foods have different amounts of calories so the recommended serving size will also vary. The right amount of food that a Pomeranian requires will vary on his age, activity level, and individual metabolism.

A good guideline about feeding the right amount of food is this. Recommended servings for puppies are 55 calories per pound while for adult Poms are 45 calories per pound.

When your Pom is undergoing a growth spurt, his appetite may increase and if he appears to want more after finishing his meal, do not hesitate to offer a second serving. It is very impossible for a growing Pom puppy to eat too much.

Protein

Pomeranians have a tiny stomach and they cannot properly digest foods with a lot of filler especially that most dog food companies use grain and plant matter as filler in their foods. Poms that do not get enough proteins may become malnourished and underweight. If you choose to buy commercial canned food, it should contain little to no filler. You can let your dog eat small amounts of boiled chicken or liver but be sure that it is cooked, as puppies' stomachs are not developed enough to digest raw food.

Dry Food

Tooth loss is very common for Pomeranians so in order to prevent it, you need to provide dry dog food which will keep your dog's teeth and gums healthy. Dry dog food to be chosen should be in small pieces so that it will be easy for tiny mouths to chew.

Treats

You cannot easily give your Pomeranians too many treats as a tiny dog has a tiny stomach. Always remember that Pomeranians should never get people food. You can give your Poms commercial treats for as long as there is no filler. This can serve as occasional treats or for positive reinforcement in training

Types of Commercial Dog Foods

Now let's discuss the three main types of commercial dog foods, which are wet, soft/moist, and dry. They are different in many aspects including moisture content, palatability, cost, and nutritional benefit.

- **Wet food**

Wet foods are usually sold in cans and contain 75 to 80 % water, 8-15% protein and 2-15% fat. Dogs eat more of this type of food without gaining weight because of the high moisture content. Canned foods, if compared to dry and soft/moist products offer the highest palatability, but wet food also has the highest cost per serving,

- **Dry Food**

Dry foods are packed in bags and contain 18-40% protein, 7-22% fat, 12-50% carbohydrates and about 10% moisture. It comes in different sizes, shapes, and colors because dog discerns the density, texture, shape and size of the food, and the way food may feel in the mouth contributes to palatability.

- **Soft or Moist Food**

This is usually sold in boxes and contains single-serving pouches. It contains approximately 15-25% protein, 5-10% fat, 25-35% carbohydrates, and approximately 30% water. This type of food is highly palatable and very convenient to serve and store.

How Often to Feed Pomeranian

The number of meals that you give to a Pom depends on his age. Feeding your dog the right amount of food can also be tricky. Below, you will know how much to feed your Pom depending on his age.

- **Brand new puppies**

    It is recommended to free-feed during the first month of your Pom, meaning, fresh food is left out at all times. This is because blood sugar can drop quickly for young puppies, and one cause of this is not eating enough amount of food.

- **Puppies 3 months to 12 years**

    In this age range, you must feed your Pomeranian puppy three times a day. You may consider buying a treat dispensing toy so that if you will be gone during the day for the mid-meal, your Pom will not miss his food.

- **Poms 1 year and older**

    Some adult Pomeranians are good with eating three times a day, while some may be happy with two meals a day. Always take note that snacks should be given in addition to these feedings. Mostly, these are reserved for rewarding and training purposes.

Tips in Selecting a High-Quality Dog Food Brand

As a pet owner, feeding your Pom a high-quality well-balanced food is one of the best things that you can do to keep your pet healthy. Picking the right food will keep your dog's hair coat sleek and shiny. It will also help strengthen his immune system and it will keep his digestive system in good health.

In order to improve your Pom's diet, start by simply ignoring the labeling claims on commercial pet food. Look instead for AAFCO certification so that you can be sure it meets the basic requirements for vitamins and trace minerals.

What to look for in a dry pet food

The first thing to look in dry pet food is meat. Dogs are carnivores and they thrive on a diet that is based on meat. Dogs do not need a lot of carbohydrates. The reason why grains and carbs are added to pet food is because they are way cheaper than meat, and they hold the kibbled bits together. They didn't add that for the sake of good nutrition for your meat-eating pet.

The quality and source of protein content in the formula are very important for your pet's health. The first thing to look for in a dog's food is the ingredient list like beef, turkey, lamb or chicken. Avoid any formula that makes use of unidentified sources, described non-specifically as meat, animal, or poultry.

How to Feed Your Pomeranian Dogs

Owning a Pom means understanding their feeding requirements. You should be knowledgeable about this because this is very important for their health. At any stages of their lives, they should be given a proper diet for their well-being and healthy growth.

If you are feeding your Pomeranian in a wrong way, it may result in some health problems. They may suffer from obesity or other diseases like strained ligaments and joints if you feed them too much. Take note that a puppy Pomeranian burns more calories quickly compared to adults. Therefore, it is very vital to understand the food requirement of your Pomeranian depending on his age.

Importance of quality food for your Poms

Cheap dog foods contain various harmful ingredients which may affect the health of your Pom in a negative way. You have to be aware that various harmful by products and fillers are present in different dog foods and these have almost zero nutrition. It is good if you can feed your Poms raw food diet.

The amount of food given to a Pom varies on the age, size, metabolism and the level of the activity of your dog. Recommended daily amount of food to a Pomeranian adult is ¼ to ½ cup of high quality dry food and these are given in two meals.

Below are the recommended servings for puppies-

- ½ cup of food for 1 pound puppy
- 1 cup of food for 3 pounds puppy
- 25 cups of food for 5 pound puppy
- 2 cups of food for 6 pounds puppy

There are changes according to requirements of the diet of pregnant, senior, and inactive Pomeranians so it is recommended consulting with the vet. Pomeranians burn more calorie compared to other breeds of dogs because they have high energy levels and require food at regular intervals. A growing Pom should be fed three to four times a day at regular intervals. When they reach adulthood, they should be fed the same amount of food twice a day.

Toxic Foods to Avoid

There are some foods that you should not feed your Poms under any occasion. The list of foods below should be carefully avoided to keep your dogs away from accidents.

- **Alcohol**

Alcoholic beverages or food products that contain alcohol may cause diarrhea, vomiting, central nervous system depression, decreased coordination, difficulty breathing, abnormal blood acidity, tremors, coma, and even death.

- **Avocado**

Dogs that might get a chance to eat avocado may cause cardiovascular damage or even death.

- **Chocolate, coffee, and caffeine**

All of these products contain substances called methylxanthines which can be found in cacao seeds. If these are ingested by dogs, they might experience diarrhea, vomiting, panting, excessive thirst and urination, abnormal heart rhythm, seizures and even death.

- **Citrus**

This can cause irritation and possibly even central nervous system depression if eaten in significant amounts.

- **Coconut and coconut oil**

This may not cause serious harm to your pet if ingested in just small amounts. But it may cause stomach upsets, loose stools or diarrhea.

- **Grapes and raisins**

These fruits can cause kidney failure although it is still not known what substance is present in grapes and raisins. Until more information is known about its toxic substance, it is still best to avoid feeding raisins and grapes to your dogs.

- **Macadamia nuts**

This can cause weakness, vomiting, depression, tremors and hyperthermia on dogs.

- **Milk and dairy**

Milk and other dairy products can cause dogs' diarrhea or other digestive problems.

- **Nuts**

Nuts contain a high amount of oils and fats that can cause vomiting and diarrhea and also pancreatitis in pets.

- **Onions, garlic, chives**

These herbs and vegetables can cause gastrointestinal irritation that could lead to red blood cell damage.

- **Raw/Undercooked Meat, Eggs, and Bones**

Raw eggs and meats may contain bacteria like Salmonella and E. coli that can be harmful not only to dogs but also to humans. On the other hand, raw bones can be very dangerous for a domestic pet that might choke on bones.

- **Salt and salty snack foods**

These can produce excessive thirst and urination, or even sodium ion poisoning for your Poms which will lead to vomiting, diarrhea, tremors, depression, elevated body temperature, seizures and even death.

- **Xylitol**

This is used as a sweetener which can cause insulin release in most dogs, which can lead to liver failure.

- **Yeast dough**

This can cause gas to accumulate in your dog's digestive system that may lead to stomach bloat, and potentially twist that may become a life threatening emergency.

Chapter Six: Maintenance for Pomeranian Dogs

Let's assume that you already have your own Pomeranian dog. The most difficult part of owning one is the responsibility that comes with it. It is necessary to provide them their basic needs and keep them healthy all the time. In this section, you will be informed about how to properly take care of your dog and how to maintain their healthy lifestyle as well as their well-being.

Tips on How to Dog-Proof Your Home

If you already purchased your Pom, you should keep in mind that you have to provide a safe environment for them. There are steps to be taken to prepare your yard and home for your dog in order to eliminate any dangers. Baby proofing your home is similar to preparing your home for a new puppy. New dogs are impertinent by nature, so they would want to investigate everything even if those things could be dangerous. Therefore, you should make sure that each room of your home is a safe environment for your pet.

- **Dog proofing bathrooms and kitchens**

Bathrooms and kitchens could be dangerous for your pets because of the cleaning supplies, medications, and other chemicals. These are the two basic rooms in your home where dog proofing is imperative. Consider the following to keep your pets safe in the bathrooms and kitchens.

- Make sure to put items like cleaning supplies, laundry soaps and medications on high shelves.
- Keep all the food out of reach from your dogs because it might be dangerous for consumption. Even if the

food does not cause a threat, the packaging could be the problem.

- Always keep trash cans covered so that your dog won't get into the garbage
- Some pets are not only curious but quite clever so consider installing childproof latches on cabinets.
- Avoid your pet from jumping into the dryer before turning it on.
- Block any small spaces such as small spaces behind the washer and dryer or holes in cabinets.
- Always keep the toilet lid down so that your pet can not drink harmful chemicals.

- **Dog proofing the living room**

Not only the kitchen and the bathroom pose most serious threats for pets but also the living room also because it contains items that could also be dangerous. In order to make sure that your pets are safe in the living room, you must consider the following:

- Move your plants out of reach from your Poms and better yet, assure that all plants in your home or yard is safe for your pet and is not poisonous to them.
- Make sure that any heating or air vents have proper covers

- Keep dangling wires from stereos, televisions, lamps and other items out of reach of your Poms
- Put away from your dogs any breakable items such as knick knacks that your Pom can knock over and break
- Put away any toys or kid games that have small pieces because this can be a choking hazard to your curious Pom.

- **Dog proof the bedroom**

The bedroom might be safe for your Poms and not a lot are needed to be done here to dog proof. However, there are still few steps that can be taken to make your bedroom safer for your Poms:

- Keep any medicine, lotion or cosmetics that are placed on a bedside table, out of reach.
- Make sure that your Poms can not access and chew any electric wires in some areas.
- Keep laundry and shoes out of reach of your Poms because buttons and strings can pose a choking hazard and potentially even more serious issues if ingested
- Make sure that your Poms are not staying or sleeping in drawers or closets before shutting them

- **Dog proof the garage and backyard**

The backyard and the garage can be home to a number of items that are risky for your Poms just as with the kitchen and bathroom. If you are thinking of leaving your Poms in the garage and backyard, you must first consider the following:

- Make sure to clean the floor of the garage so that chemicals like antifreeze are nowhere to be found. Your Pom can die if these chemicals are ingested.
- Move all chemicals in the garage to high shelves or in a closet that can't be accessed by your pets.
- Check the fence for any spaces or holes where your Pom might squeeze through and patch them up or consider boarding the spaces.

Habitat Requirements for Pomeranian Dogs

The great thing about Pomeranians is that they don't take up too much space to roam around with, but aside from space, the main thing your Pomeranian needs in terms of its habitat is lots of love and affection from his human companions and adequate daily exercise. Even though the Pomeranian is sometimes too stubborn and cutely witty, it is a very loyal and affectionate breed that bonds closely with family, so you should make an effort to spend some quality time with your Pomeranian each and every day. If your Pomeranian doesn't get enough attention he may be more likely to develop problem behaviors like chewing or excessive barking and potential aggression as well as separation anxiety.

In addition to playing with your Pomeranian and spending time with him every day, you also need to make sure that his needs for exercise are met. The Pomeranian doesn't require extensive exercises but it is still recommended to take your dog for a walk or run once in a while plus some active play time, this is very important for your Pomeranian. You should also make sure your Pomeranian gets plenty of mental stimulation from interactive toys and games.

Toys and Accessories for Pomeranian Dogs

Pom's supplies will change as each young puppy matures into an adult dog and then yet again when then also when they become a senior. The products associated with Pomeranian clearly indicate if they're appropriate for their age. When you are already ready to welcome your new Pom into your home, make sure you already have their personal supplies stocked to help keep them happy and healthy at every stage of their lives.

With the right nutrients and ingredients, Pom's food supplies can help give your Pomeranians the building blocks they need to prolong their years of face licking and tail wagging. You can also provide your Poms treats to keep them feeling rewarded, focused and excited to learn new tricks and right manners.

However, if your Poms aren't pleased by treats, you can give them a collection of dog toys for every preference. In that way, you can have a reward system for your Pom or simply just give them some much needed exercise with their plush dog ball or toys.

In addition to treating and toy fueled playtime, daily walks with your Poms' accessories can provide great bonding moments. There is a large array of Pom's accessories and clothes for every occasion and season to keep them looking comfortably stylish wherever they go.

If your Poms are new to walks, there are also specialized dog accessories that are already available to help leash train your Poms, so you can make sure your young Pom can respect the rules of the road as they explore the world outside of their homes. There are also dog training supplies available in the market to reinforce good behavior like pee pads, clickers, and bark collars.

Additionally, your Pom deserves the best bed or crating dog supplies for their size and sleeping style. Dog crate covers, heated bed products, and blankets can also make for a more comfortable good night's rest.

For your on-the-go needs of your Poms, there are also dog carriers and car seat accessories available in the market if you want to make trips to the park. Getting the right car accessories for your Poms don't just only make you hassle-free during travel, but they will also make it more comfortable and safer too.

Also, if your vet prescribes or recommends something for your pup, you must really invest on it like dog products to tackle fleas, ticks, and more.

Tips for Keeping Your Dogs Happy Indoors and Outdoors

Pomeranians are indoor dogs so they must always be kept inside our homes, in a safely fenced yard, or on-leash. But they are not inside our homes all the time. They can still go for a walk at the dog park provided they have a full supervision. This section will enumerate the tips that will help your dog stay happy whether indoors or outdoors.

Pomeranians like to see what's going on outside so why not open the curtains of your homes so they can have a foresight on the outside. Most dogs enjoy a nice view, especially when it's sunny outside, the incoming light can improve your dog's mood. Open also the windows so that your Poms can get some fresh air. But make sure to do this only if you are at home and there's someone to look after your Pom. Puzzle games are also great for a dog while they are indoors. It can be a nice pass time and can stimulate your dog's brain especially that you are not always there to play with them.

You can also try buying a treadmill for your Poms. It can be a great way to keep your Poms in good shape when you have no time to exercise them. Your dogs then can definitely exercise at home when it's convenient whether you are sick or the weather is bad. Having a bond with your dogs indoors are the best thing to do when you can't go outside for a walk. Make sure to always make time for your Poms. You may snuggle on the couch, make a brushing session, or even a massage will definitely keep them happy. You can also practice training your dog when you are inside your homes. Although it may seem boring, your Pom might enjoy this because it gives them a job and they are getting to work with you. Taking even just a small amount of time to practice tricks, obedience, etc. will keep your dog's mind sharp and will eliminate boredom.

As mentioned earlier, Pomeranian dogs are intended in indoors so it is not really recommended that he should be treated as an outdoor dog, even though he can moderately tolerate the hot and cold weather. So it's better off leaving him inside your home with your family.

You can let your Poms go outdoors like in the yard when he already reached eight weeks old. However, make sure that there are no other dogs that can get in and this includes other dogs you own. Make sure also that your yard is clean and that you have treated the ground for weeds and fleas. When your Poms reached eight weeks old, you can take them outside for as long as you hold him at all times. His feet can never touch the ground outside until he has had all the necessary shots except in your back yard if it is safe. You must avoid taking your Poms out in public areas until his puppy shots are already completed. This includes walking along the footpath, being out in your front yard, at the shops, in parks, in yards belonging to neighbors and so on. Your Poms must be 12-16 weeks old before he can be safely taken outdoors but be sure you still have his leash at all times.

It's very unhealthy to keep your dog indoors at all times. Your home won't have sufficient space for him to roam around unless you have a spacious mansion. It is necessary to give your Poms a small amount of sunshine each day for Vitamin D. Besides, getting enough exercise for your Poms is very essential. You have to plan your walks the same time each day so that he has something to look forward to. Exercises are important because it helps him get off diseases and he could be able to smell, hear and see new things. This makes his hearth healthy and balances out his muscle tone.

Chapter Seven: Showing Your Pomeranian

The Pomeranian is a wonderful dog to keep as a pet but this breed has the potential to be so much more than that. These dogs are very clever, active and trainable which makes them a great choice as a show dog.

In order to show your Pomeranian, however, you have to make sure that he meets the requirements for the breed standard and you need to learn the basics about showing dogs. In this chapter you will receive information about the breed standard for Pomeranian breeds and you will find general information about preparing your dog for show.

Pomeranian Breed Standard

The Pomeranian is an alert and enthusiastic breed that is accepted and recognized by the American Kennel Club (AKC). This section will give you the breed standard and general guidelines on how to present your dog.

Official Pomeranian Standard

General Appearance

The Pomeranian is a small breed dog that is from Nordic descent. The breed generally has a double coat; it has a short undercoat, and a long outer coat that has quite a rough texture. It has a naturally inquisitive look and portrays a clever and commanding aura.

Height and Weight
- Weight and height should be in proportion to the overall size and structure

Head
- The head is balanced with the body
- It is broad at the back tapering to the nose to form a wedge

Eyes and Eye Color

- Medium in size, almond shaped, proportionate with other facial features
- Eyes are bright and dark in color
- Has black rims

Skull and Muzzle

- The skull should be slightly round but not domed
- The muzzle should be short and straight
- The ratio of length of the muzzle to skull should be ⅓ to ⅔.
- The muzzle should not be coarse

Expression

- The expression should be fox-like, or must have that alert and curious look

Nose

- Should be black in color (except self-colored in chocolate, beaver and blue)

Ears

- Small and erect
- Must be proportional to the head (ear set proportion should be favored over its size)

Teeth and Bite

- A one tooth alignment is acceptable
- The bite should be scissors

Neck, Back and Chest

- The neck should be set well and proportional to the shoulders
- The chest should be oval in shape
- Back and loin should be short and strongly coupled with some tuck-up
- The croup should be flat

Body

- Should be compact, proportionate and well-ribbed
- The topline should be of level from withers to croup

Legs

- **Forequarters:** The shoulders are well laid back
- The shoulder blade and upper arm length must be equal.
- The elbows should be held close to the body and turn neither in nor out.
- Legs when viewed from the front should be moderately spaced, straight and parallel to each other. It must be set well behind the forechest.
- The height from withers to elbows approximately equals height from ground to elbow.
- The shoulders and legs should be moderately muscled.
- **Hindquarters**: The angulation of the hindquarters should be similar in degree to that of the forequarters
- The buttocks should be well behind the set of the tail.
- The thighs should be moderately muscled.
- The upper thigh and lower leg length should be equal.
- Stifles must be strong, moderately bent and clearly defined.
- Legs - when viewed from the rear must be straight
- Declaws may also be removed

Feet

- **Front Feet:** must be round, tight, appearing cat-like, and well-arched. It should be compact, it must be standing well up on toes
- **Rear Feet:** same standards as the front feet

Tail

- The tail is preferably well plumed, sets high but flat and may be carried over the back

Coat

- The coat should form a ruff around the neck, framing the head, extending over the shoulders and chest
- Forelegs should be well-feathered.
- Thighs and hind legs should be heavily coated to the hock forming a skirt
- A cotton type coat is undesirable in an adult.
- The coat should be in good and healthy condition especially the skirt, tail, and undercarriage

Body Color

- All colors, patterns, and variations there-of are allowed and must be judged on an equal basis.

- Acceptable colors: Brindle, Parti, Piebald, Extreme Piebald, Irish and Tan.
- For specialty shows may be divided depending on their colors such as Red, Orange, Cream, and Sable; Open Black, Brown, and Blue; Open Any Other Color, Pattern, or Variation

Gait

- Gait must be smooth, balanced and brisk
- Head carriage should be carried high and proud
- The topline should remain firm and level with the overall balance maintained.

Disqualifications

- **Eyes:** light blue, blue marbled, blue flecked
- **Tail:** low tail set
- **Forequarters:** down in pasterns
- **Hindquarters:** cowhocks, knees turning in or out or lack of soundness in legs or stifles
- **Coat:** soft, flat or open coat
- **Color:** Distinct white on whole foot or on one or more whole feet (except white or parti) on any acceptable color or pattern

Tips on Preparing Your Pomeranian for Show

Once you've determined that your Pomeranian achieved all the requirements of the breed standard, and then you can think about entering him in a dog show. Dog shows occur all year-round in many different locations so check the AKC or Kennel Club website for shows in your area. Remember, the rules for each show will be different so make sure to do your research so that you and your Pomeranian are properly prepared for the show.

Here are some things you need to keep in mind while prepping your dog for show:

- Make sure that your Pomeranian has been housetrained completely before registering him for a show.

- Ensure that your dog is properly socialized to be in an environment with many other dogs and people.

- Make sure that your Pomeranian has had at least basic obedience training. He needs to respond to your commands and follow your lead in the show ring.

- Research the requirements for the individual show and make sure your Pomeranian meets them before you register.

- Take your Pomeranian to the vet to ensure that he is healthy enough for show and that he is caught up on his vaccinations – the bordatella vaccine is especially important since he'll be around a lot of other dogs.

- Pack a bag of supplies for things that you and your Pomeranian are likely to need at the show.

- Have your Pomeranian groomed the week of the show and take steps to make sure his coat stays in good condition.

Quick Checklist

Here are some things that may come in handy before, during and after the show:

- Registration information
- Dog crate or exercise pen
- Grooming table and grooming supplies
- Food and treats
- Food and water bowls
- Trash bags
- Medication (if needed)

- Change of clothes
- Food/water for self
- Paper towels or rags
- Toys for the dog

Chapter Eight: Breeding Your Pomeranian Dogs

Are you prepared in breeding your Pomeranian dog? One must be fully prepared before breeding. Do you have enough money to do this? This is because breeding involves many veterinarian bills. Do you have time? Newborn puppies need to have a careful eye on them around the clock. Do you have the emotional strength? Even the best breeders experience loss.

Read on if you really want to become a breeder but take note that there are a lot of things that you should know. This chapter will give you an idea of breeding one.

Basic Dog Breeding Information

The first rule that to you have to understand and follow is that breeding is best left to professional breeders. But of course, it is also essential that you know the basics of breeding a dog. A lot of things are involved, and it is important that you know your responsibilities and all the things that you need to observe to ensure that the breeding will produce healthy pom puppies.

There is somewhat a high level of loss in puppies. This is caused by different kinds of reasons, and can also happen in any breed not only on Poms, but this happens more often in toy breeds. Anyone who is breeding must understand and accept that puppies may die inexplicably at times. It is heartbreaking and tragic of course.

Mating Behavior of dogs

When a female dog or what they termed it as the 'bitch' is in heat, there are a few signs that can point towards her beginning this process. These are:

- Being nervous
- Easily spooked
- Easily distracted

- Urinating more than usual

Her personality may also alter due to the abrupt change in her hormones. Male dogs are ready to breed from the age of 18 months to 4/5 years old according to breeding dogs Info center. An interesting fact about male dogs is that when they hit the age around 10 years old, the semen they produce will not be capable of impregnating a female.

Ovulation Timing

A lot of breeders today use lab tests to measure Progesterone, vaginal cytology, and luteinizing hormone to determine when ovulation occurs. Breeders know that the cycle is usually 21 days despite what some male dogs think. What may be normal for one dog may differ from another. Some bitches' cycle on schedule, while others mate and ovulate from 12-21 days. Some have 'clear heats', false or flaky seasons, or even false pregnancies. Here are the average estrus changes an owner may expect in normal heat cycles.

- **Day 1:** Attention to rear and licking. Discharge is bright or dark red color, swelling of the vulva. You can start counting heat cycle from when the blood hits the ground.

- **Day 2 – 7:** Bright red discharge with swelling increases

- **Day 8 – 10:** The color begins to lighten and turn into pinkish. Swelling is at peak and the vulva has a spongy feel and look.

- **Day 9 – 14:** The color changes from light pink to clear or straw colored. The swelling is down and the vulva may appear hard or dry on edges.

- **Day 14 – 21:** Color clears, discharge and swelling is almost gone and bitch may already act receptive, but is still snappy. You can count 58-62 days for puppies! But there also exceptions to the rule. Some bitched may mate and conceive as late as 22 days.

Tips for Breeding Your Pomeranian

Now that you know the basics about breeding dogs you can learn the specifics about Pomeranian. The Pomeranian has a gestation period lasting about 58 - 68 days (or about 9 to 10 weeks). The gestation period is the period of time following conception during which the puppies develop in the mother's uterus. The average litter size for the Pomeranian breed is between 5 to 6 puppies. Keep in mind that new mothers will often have smaller litters – the next few litters will generally be larger before the litter size starts to taper off again.

To increase your chances of a successful breeding, you need to keep track of your Pomeranian's estrus cycle. Once your female reaches the point of ovulation, you can introduce her to the male dog and let nature take its course. Breeding behavior varies slightly from one breed to another, but you can expect the male dog to mount the female from behind (as long as she is receptive). If the breeding is successful, conception will occur and the gestation period will begin.

While the puppies are developing inside your female Pomeranian's uterus, you need to take special care to make sure the female is properly nourished. You do not need to make changes to your dog's diet until the fourth or fifth week of pregnancy. At that point you should slightly increase her daily rations in an amount proportionate to her weight gain. It is generally best to offer your dog free feeding because she will know how much she needs to eat. Make sure your dog's diet is high in protein as well as calories and fat to support the development of her puppies – calcium is also very important.

<u>Signs that your dog is pregnant:</u>

- Fast nipple growth or appearance
- Less energetic
- More affectionate or clingy
- Experiences mood swings
- The stomach will expand and get firm
- The dog will clean herself more than the usual
- May attempt to build a dog's nest.

Labor Process of Pomeranian

By the eighth week of pregnancy you should start preparing yourself and your dog for the whelping. This is the time when you should set up a whelping box where your female dog can comfortably give birth to her puppies. Place the box in a quiet, dim area and line it with newspapers and old towels for comfort. The closer it gets to the whelping, the more time your dog will spend in the whelping box, preparing it for her litter.

During the last week of your Pomeranian's pregnancy you should start taking her internal temperature at least once per day – this is the greatest indicator of impending labor. The normal body temperature for a dog is about 100°F to 102°F (37.7°C to 38.8°C). When your dog's body temperature drops, you can expect contractions to begin within 24 hours or so. Prior to labor, your dog's body temperature may drop as low as 98°F (36.6°C) – if it gets any lower, contact your veterinarian.

Once your Pomeranian starts going into labor, you can expect her to show some obvious signs of discomfort. Your dog might start pacing restlessly, panting, and switching positions. The early stages of labor can often last for several hours and contractions may occur as often as 10 minutes apart. If your Pomeranian has contractions for more than 2 hours without any of the puppies being born, contact your veterinarian immediately. Once your dog starts giving birth, the puppies will arrive about every thirty minutes following ten to thirty minutes of straining.

After each puppy is born, the Pomeranian will lick the puppy clean; it may even eat the umbilical cord because it is animal instinct. This also helps to stimulate the puppy to start breathing on his own. Once all of the puppies have been born, the mother will expel the rest of the placenta (the afterbirth) and then let the puppies start nursing. It is essential that the puppies begin nursing within one hour of being born because this is when they will receive the colostrum from the mother. Colostrum is the first milk produced and it contains a variety of nutrients as well as antibodies to protect the pups until their own immune systems have time to develop. In addition to making sure that the puppies are feeding, you should also make sure that the mother eats soon after whelping.

Pomeranian puppies are small in size; these puppies are also born blind, with their eyes and ears closed, so they are completely dependent on the mother for several weeks. Around 3rd week, the puppies will open their eyes and their ears will become erect sometime after. As the puppies grow, they will start to become increasingly active and the will grow very quickly as long as they are properly fed by the mother.

At six weeks of age is the time you should begin weaning the puppies by offering them small amounts of puppy food soaked in water or broth. The puppies might sample small bits of solid food even while they are still nursing and the mother will general wean the puppies by week 8, with or without your help. If you plan to sell the puppies, be sure not to send them home unless they are fully weaned at least 8 weeks old. You should also take steps to start socializing the puppies from an early age to make sure they turn into well-adjusted adults.

Chapter Nine: Keeping Your Dog Healthy

It's you Pom's life – and as a pet owner, your responsibility is to make sure that their life is long, happy and healthy as possible. Are you already prepared to keep you Poms happy and healthy in a long term? In this section, you will find tons of tips on how to maintain your dog happy and healthy. Information about common health problems is also addressed in this section.

Common Health Problems

Pomeranians are very healthy, hardy and long-lived type of breed. However, despite this, they still have a relative health issues. The Pom, just like other breeds do have some common health problems. It is important as a pet owner, to be conscientious of your Pom's health at all times, not only when he seems to be not feeling well or has developed an issue. Regular checking your Poms is a very important step in catching problems early as possible. This applies to Poms of all ages whether it is puppies, adults or seniors.

Health Issues Seen With the Pomeranian Breed

The Pomeranian is also prone to certain canine diseases and health problems just like any other dogs. But this does not mean that your Pom will develop these heath issues. The following are the health problems most common to Pomeranians.

Cataracts

Canine cataracts are the most common problems affecting the dog's eye. Toy dogs, like the Pomeranian are more prone to this sickness. This health issue can appear at any age, from when the Pomeranian is born up until he becomes older, senior dog.

Collapsed Trachea

This is also common to Pomeranian dogs. Some of this may be because of genetics, but this can be prevented in most cases. The trachea or the windpipe is supported by rings that are made up of cartilage. This cartilage is prone to injury with toy breeds. With regards to trauma related collapsed trachea, it is often due to the use of a collar instead of harness

Skin Problems

Pomeranians are prone to skin issues. Skin becomes dry and itchy. There are some remedies that can be followed in order to avoid these kinds of health problems.

Distichiasis

This is when eyelashes grow out of place; often nudging into the dog's eye. This should be treated immediately because if this is prolonged, irritation of the lash into the Pomeranian's eye can actually cause a tear to the cornea.

Entropion

This happens when a dog's eyelid edge rolls inward. This can occur any age and more often than not, this usually happens to the Pom's lower eyelids.

Hypoglycemia

This health issue is usually sudden drop in blood sugar levels. This can be very dangerous and sometimes can be fatal. This commonly happens to puppies under the age of 3 months old.

Luxating Patella

This is an issue affecting the Knee Joint. It can be usually seen in toy breed dogs like the Pomeranian. This is a condition of a kneecap and can occur because of malformation of the bone from an injury.

Pituitary Dwarfism

This is common to toy breed dogs. It happens when there is a lack of growth hormones in the body. The growth hormones not only affect the growth of a dog, but they also control the condition of the dog's bones, fur and teeth.

Seizures

Any dog may be born with a seizure condition, including a Pomeranian. It may develop as the dog grows older. It might be scary to watch a Pom go through an episode associated with this.

Skin and coat issues

Allergies can affect at about 20% of all dogs. This can cause skin issues such as peeling, itchy, dry or irritated skin.

In some cases, there may be hot spots that lead to the thinning of the hair.

Recommended Vaccinations for Pomeranian Dogs

All dogs, including Pomeranians need shots or vaccinations to certain doggy diseases. Your vet will be making a recommendation, but normally, your Pom will get the same thing at the same age as the big dogs.

Puppy shots

Never neglect to get your Pom a shot even it seems that he is too small to have one because this is vital to their health. Pom puppies first get their shots as soon as they leave their mommies. If you get your dog from a breeder at eight to nine weeks old, it is assumed that he already got a shot – even six –week- old puppies can be given a vaccination. When puppies get boosters, they get a natural immunity from their moms but it interferes with the shots that you gave to them. The protection of the moms to her obvious when that actually happens. The best thing to do is give your Pomeranian puppy a series of shots to make sure he's covered when he needs it. Pomeranians should be getting boosters every two to four weeks until he's 16 weeks old. As soon as he is finished with puppy shots, give your

Poms booster shots once every three years but if your vet recommends annual boosters, follow it and go with that schedule.

Below table summarizes the different vaccinations that can be given to your Pomeranian. You can review it so you have an idea what shots to give to your dogs.

In this section you will learn the vaccination schedule that your puppy or dog may need, but be sure to consult the veterinarian for further instructions.

Vaccination Schedule for Dogs			
Vaccine	**Doses**	**Age**	**Booster**
Rabies	1	12 weeks	annual
Distemper	3	6-16 weeks	3 years
Parvovirus	3	6-16 weeks	3 years
Adenovirus	3	6-16 weeks	3 years
Parainfluenza	3	6 weeks, 12-14 weeks	3 years
Bordatella	1	6 weeks	annual
Lyme Disease	2	9, 13-14 weeks	annual
Leptospirosis	2	12 and 16 weeks	annual
Canine Influenza	2	6-8, 8-12 weeks	annual

Signs of Possible Illnesses

- **Sneezing** - does your dog have nose discharge?
- **Dehydration** -does your dog drink less than the usual? It may be a sign that there is something wrong with your dog
- **Obesity** -is your dog showing signs of obesity? It may be prone to a heart disease, or diabetes. Monitor your dog's weight before it's too late.
- **Elimination** -does your dog regularly urinate and defecate? Always check its litter to make sure that its stool and urine is normal. Contact the vet immediately if there are any signs of bleed and diarrhea.
- **Vomiting** - does your dog vomits and is it showing signs of appetite loss?
- **Coat** -does its coat and skin still feel soft, firm and rejuvenated? If your dog is sick sometimes, it appears physically on its body.
- **Paws/Limbs** -does your dog have trouble walking or is it only dragging its legs? It could be a sign of paralysis.
- **Eyes** - are there any discharge in the eyes?
- **Overall Physique** - does your dog stays active or are there any signs of weakness and deterioration?

Emergency Guide

Accidents do happen and we cannot avoid them. When there are medical emergencies that befall our dogs, pet parents may find it difficult to make rational decisions, especially when it occurs in the middle of the night. That is why it is very important that we know what to do and should have an emergency plan in place – before we need it.

Signs Your Pet May Need Emergency Care

There are a lot of reasons when your dog needs an emergency care like a severe trauma – caused by accident or fall – choking, insect sting, heatstroke, household poisoning or other life – threatening circumstances. Below are some signs that emergency care is necessary.

- Pale gums
- Rapid breathing
- Weak or rapid pulse
- Change in body temperature
- Difficulty standing
- Apparent paralysis

- Loss of consciousness

- Seizures

- Excessive bleeding

Next steps

Dogs that are severely injured may be aggressive toward their owners, so it is very important to first protect yourself from injury.

Approach your dog calmly and slowly, kneel down and say his name. If the dog is aggressive, call for immediate help. If he is passive, fashion a makeshift stretcher and gently carry him onto it. Be sure to support his neck and back in case he is suffering any spinal injuries.

First Aid Treatments that can be performed at Home

A lot of medical emergencies require immediate veterinary care, but first aid methods may help in stabilizing your pet for transportation.

- If the dog is suffering from bleeding because of trauma, try to elevate and apply pressure to the wound
- If your pet is choking, place your fingers inside his mouth and see if you can remove the blockage

- If you cannot remove the foreign object, perform a modified Heimlich maneuver by giving a sharp rap to his chest, which will dislodge the object.

Performing CPR on your Pet

CPR may be important if your pet remains unconscious after you have removed the object that chokes him. Check first to see if he is still breathing. If not, place him on his side and perform an artificial respiration by extending his neck and head, holding his jaws closed and by blowing into his nostrils once every 3 seconds. Be sure that no air escapes between your mouth and the nose of your pet. If you really cannot hear a heartbeat, incorporate a cardiac massage, while having artificial respiration – three quick, firm chest compression for every respiration until your dog can breath normally already.

What to do if your Pom eats something Poisonous

If you think your Pom has ingested a toxic food or substance, call your vet immediately or the ASPCA Animal Poison Control Center's 24-hour hotline at (888) 426 – 4435. They will make a recommendation, and will consider the age and health of your dog and what and how he ate. This may include inducing vomiting, based on their assessment.

Pomeranian Dogs Care Sheet

Be grateful that you have reached this point in this book. It just means that you already know the basic information on how to take care of a Pomeranian dog and how to maintain their health and well-being. You now can be a great owner and finish this milestone is something to brag about. I am sure you have learned a lot upon finishing this book but be sure that you will apply it properly to your furry Pom. This chapter will give a summary of the things that you have learned from this book and a brief overview on how to keep your pet happy and comfortable with you and the other members of your family.

Basic Dog Information

Pedigree: Companion dogs

AKC Group: Toy Group

Breed Size: Small

Height: 8 -11 inches (20 – 28 cm)
Weight: 3 -7 pounds (1.36 – 3 kg)

Coat Length: double coated, thick

Coat Texture: silky, smooth and fine

Color: blue, blue and tan, black, black and tan, chocolate, chocolate and tan, orange, orange sable, cream, cream sable, red, red sable, white or brindle

Ears: small, fluffy

Tail: feathered, long, curled

Temperament: extrovert loves to socialize, loyal, caring

Strangers: generally friendly with strangers as long as there is proper introduction

Other Dogs: generally good with other dogs if properly trained and socialized; may tend to launched itself to larger dogs

Other Pets: friendly with other pets but if not properly introduce may result to potential aggression

Training: active, smart and can be easily trained

Exercise Needs: very active; doesn't require regular or excessive amount of exercise

Health Conditions: cataracts, collapsed trachea, skin problems, distichiasis, entropion, hypoglycemia, luxating patella, pituitary dwarfism, seizues, skin and coat issues

Lifespan: 12 -15 years

Habitat Requirements

Recommended Accessories: crate, dog bed, food/water dishes, toys, collar, leash, harness, grooming supplies

Collar and Harness: sized by weight

Grooming Supplies: soft brittle brush, nail clipper

Grooming Frequency: occasional brushing; professional grooming at least 2 times a year (depending on your dog)

Energy Level: relatively high

Exercise Requirements: at least once a day plus active playtime

Crate: highly recommended

Crate Size: just large enough for dog to lie down and turn around comfortably

Crate Extras: lined with blanket or plush pet bed

Food/Water: preferably stainless steel or ceramic bowls

Toys: start with an assortment, see what the dog likes; include some mentally stimulating toys

Training: play games to give your dog extra exercise during the day; train your dog for various dog sports

Nutritional Needs

Nutritional Needs: protein, carbohydrates, fats, vitamins and minerals, water

Amount to Feed (puppy): 10 grams

Amount to Feed (adult): 12.5 grams

Important Minerals:
  Vitamin A (Retinol, beta carotene as precursor)
  Vitamin D (Calciferol)
  Vitamin E (Tocopherol)
  Vitamin K (Naphthoquinone)
  Vitamin B1 (Thiamine)

Vitamin B2 (Riboflavin)

Vitamin B3 (Niacin)

Vitamin B5 (Pantothenic Acid)

Amount to Feed

½ cup of food for 1 pound puppy

1 cup of food for 3 pounds puppy

25 cups of food for 5 pound puppy

2 cups of food for 6 pounds puppy

Dog Food Types:

Dry: 75 to 80 % water, 8-15% protein and 2-15% fat

Semimoist: 15-25% protein, 5-10% fat, 25-35% carbohydrates, and approximately 30% water

Canned: 75% moisture

Food Additives: Antioxidants, Herbs, Flavors and Extracts

Feeding Amount: recommended daily amount of food to a Pomeranian adult is ¼ to ½ cup of high quality dry food and these are given in two meals

Breeding Information

Menstruation period: two to three weeks

Sexual Maturity (female): 5-12 months

Sexual Maturity (male): 5 months

Breeding Age (female): 14 months

Breeding Age (male): 16 months

Breeding Type: usually twice a year

Litter Size: about 5-6 puppies

Birth Interval: 15 – 30 minutes

Gestation Period: 58 - 63 days

Kitten Birth Weight: 75g to 350g

Signs of Labor: body temperature drops below normal 100° to 102°F (37.7° to 38.8°C), may be as low as 98°F (36.6°C); dog begins nesting in a dark, quiet place

Contractions: period of 10 minutes in waves of 3 to 5 followed by a period of rest

Whelping: puppies are born in 1/2 hour increments following 10 to 30 minutes of forceful straining

Puppies: born with eyes and ears closed; eyes open at 3 weeks, teeth develop at 10 weeks

Weaning: start offering puppy food soaked in water at 6 weeks; fully weaned by 8 weeks

Socialization: start as early as possible to prevent puppies from being nervous as an adult

Index

C

D

H

I

K

L

M

N

O

P

Q

R

S

W

Photo Credits

Page 1 Photo by user Megu via Flickr.com, <https://www.flickr.com/photos/kenkenranran/6339329981>

Page 10 Photo by user paulwolf2012 via Flickr.com, <https://www.flickr.com/photos/77360717@N03/>

Page 19 Photo by user nancy odchigue via Flickr.com, <https://www.flickr.com/photos/asian_hotfruity/484301828>

Page 23 Photo by user Megu via Flickr.com, <https://www.flickr.com/photos/kenkenranran/19585186340 >

Page 27 Photo by user kitty043 via Flickr.com, <https://www.flickr.com/photos/kitty043/2677061633>

Page 38 Photo by user Guan's Family via Flickr.com, <https://www.flickr.com/photos/guans_family/3625220427>

Page 54 Photo by user Ming Chan via Flickr.com, <https://www.flickr.com/photos/sir_mencius/3040616378>

Page 65 Photo by user Charlene Smith via Flickr.com, <https://www.flickr.com/photos/85993469@N08/12621751824 in>

References

"**10 Not-So-Fluffy Facts about Pomeranians**"
<http://mentalfloss.com/article/72441/10-not-so-fluffy-facts-about-pomeranians>

"**10 Ways to Tell If Your Dog is Healthy**"
<http://www.readersdigest.ca/home-garden/pets/10-ways-tell-if-your-dog-is-healthy/10/ >

"**12 Tips for A Healthy, Happy Indoor Dog**"
< http://iheartdogs.com/12-tips-for-a-healthy-happy-indoor-dog/3/>

"**AAFCO Dog Food Nutrient Profiles**"
DogFoodAdvisor.com
<http://www.dogfoodadvisor.com/frequently-asked-questions/aafco-nutrient-profiles/>

"**Annual Dog Care Costs**" PetFinder.com
<https://www.petfinder.com/pet-adoption/dog-adoption/annual-dog-care-costs/>

"Choosing a Healthy Puppy" WebMD
<http://pets.webmd.com/dogs/guide/choosing-healthy-
   puppy>

"How to Find a Responsible Breeder" HumaneSociety.org
   <http://www.humanesociety.org/issues/puppy_mills/tips/f
   inding_responsible_dog_breeder.html?referrer=https://ww
   w.google.com/>

"How to train Pomeranians"
<https://www.petcarerx.com/article/how-to-train-
pomeranians/436>

"My Bowl: What Goes into a Balanced Diet for Your Dog?"
   PetMD.com
<http://www.petmd.com/dog/slideshows/
   nutrition-center/my-bowl-what-goes-into-a-balanced-diet-
   for-your-dog>

"Nutrients Your Dog Needs" ASPCA.org
<https://www.aspca.org/pet-care/dog-care/nutrients-your-
   dog-needs>

"Nutrition: General Feeding Guidelines for Dogs"
VCAAnimalHospitals.com
<http://www.vcahospitals.com/main/pet-health-
information/article/animal-health/nutrition-general-
feeding-guidelines-for-dogs/6491>

"Official Breed Standard of Pomeranians" AKC.org
<http://images.akc.org/pdf/breeds/standards/Pomeranian.pd
f?_ga=1.200648878.186202706.1485301797>

"People Foods to Avoid Feeding Your Pets"
<http://www.aspca.org/pet-care/animal-poison-
control/people-foods-avoid-feeding-your-pets >
"Pet Care Costs" ASPCA.org
<https://www.aspca.org/adopt/pet-care-costs>

"Pomeranian"
<http://www.dogbreedinfo.com/pomeranian.htm>

"Pomeranian Behavior"
<http://www.petpom.com/pomeranian-behavior>

"Pomeranian Breeders"
<http://www.petpom.com/pomeranian-breeders>

"Pomeranian Health Issues"
<http://www.petpom.com/pomeranian-health >

"Pomeranian - Physical Characteristics"
<http://www.petwave.com/Dogs/Breeds/Pomeranian/Appearance.aspx>

"Pomeranian, Pom, Pom Pom, Deutsche Spitze, Zwergspitz, Spitz Nain, Spitz Enano, and Zwers"
< http://dogs.petbreeds.com/l/123/Pomeranian>
"Pomeranian Temperament What's Good About 'Em, What's Bad About 'Em"
<http://www.yourpurebredpuppy.com/reviews/pomeranians.html>

"Pros and Cons of Owning a Pomeranian"
<http://www.yogispomcentral.com/pros-cons-owning-pomeranian/>

"Puppy Proofing Your Home" Hill's Pet.com
<http://www.hillspet.com/dog-care/puppy-proofing-your-home.html>

"Puppy Proofing Your Home" PetEducation.com
<http://www.peteducation.com/article.cfm?c=2+2106&aid=3283>

"The Diets of Pomeranians"
<http://pets.thenest.com/diets-pomeranians-12754.html>

"Vitamins and Minerals Your Dog Needs" Kim Boatman
   TheDogDaily.com
<http://www.thedogdaily.com/dish/diet/dogs_vitamins/inde
   x.html#.VHOtMPnF_IA>

Feeding Baby
Cynthia Cherry
978-1941070000

Axolotl
Lolly Brown
978-0989658430

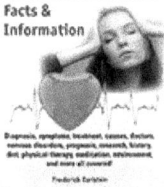

Dysautonomia, POTS
Syndrome
Frederick Earlstein
978-0989658485

Degenerative Disc
Disease Explained
Frederick Earlstein
978-0989658485

Sinusitis, Hay Fever,
Allergic Rhinitis Explained
Frederick Earlstein
978-1941070024

Wicca
Riley Star
978-1941070130

Zombie Apocalypse
Rex Cutty
978-1941070154

Capybara
Lolly Brown
978-1941070062

Eels As Pets
Lolly Brown
978-1941070167

Scabies and Lice Explained
Frederick Earlstein
978-1941070017

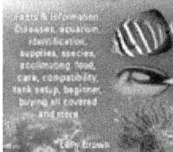

Saltwater Fish As Pets
Lolly Brown
978-0989658461

Torticollis Explained
Frederick Earlstein
978-1941070055

Kennel Cough
Lolly Brown
978-0989658409

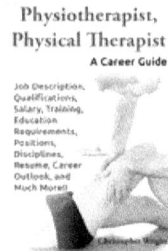

Physiotherapist, Physical
Therapist
Christopher Wright
978-0989658492

Rats, Mice, and Dormice
As Pets
Lolly Brown
978-1941070079

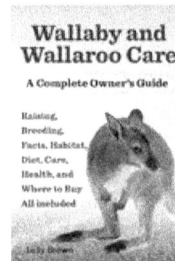

Wallaby and Wallaroo Care
Lolly Brown
978-1941070031

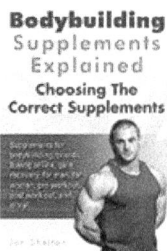

Bodybuilding Supplements
Explained
Jon Shelton
978-1941070239

Demonology
Riley Star
978-19401070314

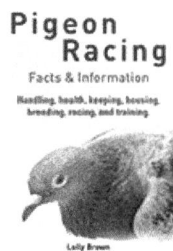

Pigeon Racing
Lolly Brown
978-1941070307

Dwarf Hamster
Lolly Brown
978-1941070390

Cryptozoology
Rex Cutty
978-1941070406

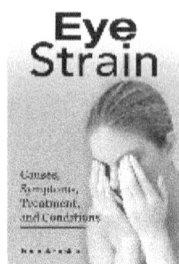

Eye Strain
Frederick Earlstein
978-1941070369

Inez The Miniature Elephant
Asher Ray
978-1941070353

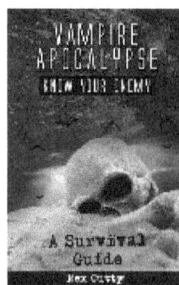

Vampire Apocalypse
Rex Cutty
978-1941070321

www.ingramcontent.com/pod-product-compliance
Lightning Source LLC
LaVergne TN
LVHW051640080426
835511LV00016B/2413